California
Native Peoples

Stephen Feinstein

Heinemann Library
Chicago, Illinois

www.heinemannraintree.com
Visit our website to find out more information about Heinemann-Raintree books.

To order:
☎ Phone 888-454-2279
💻 Visit www.heinemannraintree.com to browse our catalog and order online.

Edited by Megan Cotugno
Designed by Ryan Frieson, Kim Miracle and Betsy Wernert
Picture research by Tracy Cummins
Originated by Heinemann Library
Printed and bound in China by Leo paper Group

13 12 11 10 09
10 9 8 7 6 5 4 3 2 1

New edition ISBNS: 978-1-4329-2675-5 (hardcover)
                   978-1-4329-2682-3 (paperback)

Library of Congress Cataloging-in-Publication Data
Feinstein, Stephen.
   California Native peoples / by Stephen Feinstein.
      p. cm. -- (State studies)
   Summary: Provides an overview the daily lives of California's native peoples, profiling their arrival in the area, survival in harsh times, relationships with the environment, rituals, customs, and beliefs.
   Includes bibliographical references and index.
   ISBN 1-40340-341-4 -- ISBN 1-40340-558-1 (pbk.)
   1. Indians of North America--California--History--Juvenile literature. 2. Indians of North America--California--Social life and customs--Juvenile literature. [1. Indians of North America--California.] I. Title. II. Series: State studies (Heinemann Library (Firm))
   E78.C15F45 2002
   979.4004'97--dc21

2002010886

T 14753

Acknowledgments
The author and publishers are grateful to the following for permission to reproduce copyright material:

Cover photograph of Achomawi mother and child reproduced with permission of Edward S. Curtis/©Library of Congress.

pp. 4, 30, 40, 44 maps.com/Heinemann Library; p. 5 Derek Lucas/Museum of London/Heritage Image; p. 6 Tom Bean/ Corbis; p. 7 Eda Rogers; p. 9 Catherine Karnow/ Corbis; pp. 10, 24 National Museum of the American Indian; pp. 11B, 13, 15, 18, 22, 25 Marilyn "Angel" Wynn/NativeStock. com; p. 11T The British Museum/Heritage Image; p. 12 Merriam (C. Hart) Collection of Native American Photographs/California Heritage Collection/The Bancroft Library/University of California, Berkeley; p. 14 Phoebe Hearst Museum of Anthropology/University of California, Berkeley; pp. 16, 27B San Diego Museum of Man; p. 17 The Bancroft Library/University of California, Berkeley; pp. 19, 28, 35 Corbis; p. 20T Chuck Mitchell; pp. 20B, 39 Ben Klaffke; p. 21 Eliot Cohen; p. 23 Christie's Images/Corbis; pp. 26 Phil Schermeister/Corbis; p. 27T Richard Wagner; p. 29 Northwestern University Library, Edward S. Curtis's 'The North American Indian: The Photographic Images,' 2001/ Library of Congress; p. 31 David Muench/Corbis; p. 32 North Wind Picture Archives; p. 33 Stoddard's Lectures X, John L. Stoddard, 1898; p. 34 San Bernardino County Museum; p. 36 Bettmann/Corbis; p. 37 Bettmann/Corbis; p. 41 Phil Schermeister/Corbis; p. 42 AP Wide World Photos; p. 43 Richard Cummins/Corbis

Every effort has been made to contact copyright holders of any material reproduced in this book. Any omissions will be rectified in subsequent printings if notice is given to the publisher.

All the Internet addresses (URLs) given in this book were valid at the time of going to press. However, due to the dynamic nature of the Internet, some addresses may have changed, or sites may have changed or ceased to exist since publication. While the author and Publishers regret any inconvenience this may cause readers, no responsibility for any such changes can be accepted by either the author or the Publishers.

Contents

Some words are shown in bold, **like this**. You can find out what they mean by looking in the glossary.

First Peoples of California

Native Americans were the first people to live in California, and many still live in the state today. But how did they first get there?

During the last **Ice Age**, thick sheets of ice buried much of present-day North America. A **land bridge** stretched across the Bering Strait, which now separates Asia from Alaska. Scientists believe that about 40,000 years ago, people began to move from what is now Asia to present-day North America. They crossed the land bridge and became the first people to reach what we now call the North American continent.

Migration Routes

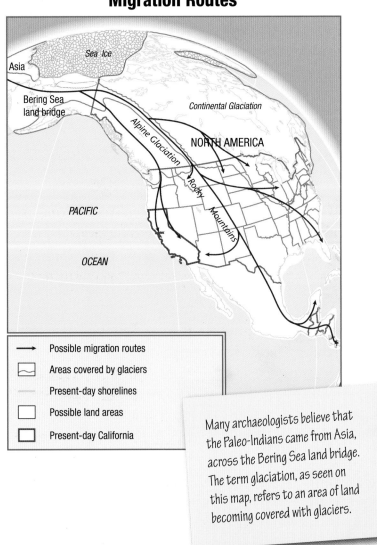

→ Possible migration routes

⌇ Areas covered by glaciers

Present-day shorelines

▢ Possible land areas

▢ Present-day California

Many archaeologists believe that the Paleo-Indians came from Asia, across the Bering Sea land bridge. The term glaciation, as seen on this map, refers to an area of land becoming covered with glaciers.

A nomadic people, the Paleo-Indians hunted animals such as the now-extinct woolly mammoth.

Nomadic Hunters of the Ice Age

Archaeologists refer to the first Americans as Paleo-Indians, the **ancestors** of today's Native Americans. Paleo-Indians were **nomadic hunters**, following herds of wild animals from place to place. Some of the animals they hunted are now **extinct**, such as the mastodon and woolly mammoth, a relative of the elephant.

Over thousands of years, groups of Paleo-Indians gradually moved south and east throughout present-day North and South America. Some archaeologists believe that during the Ice Age these people probably did not enter what is now California. These archaeologists say **glaciers** covering California's mountains and high valleys might have cut off any approach over land. However, other archaeologists believe that a small number of people may have reached California during the Ice Age. Researchers continue to study and learn about these early people and how they might have migrated to California.

Settling in California

About 14,000 years ago, the Ice Age ended. At that time, glaciers began to melt as the **climate** grew warmer. A land route free of ice opened up from Alaska southward through western Canada. Groups of people followed this route south into California. Other groups moved into California from the east by crossing the the Sierra Nevada. Still, others entered California from the deserts to the southeast. Most of California's early peoples arrived between 10,000 and 6000 BCE. However, some groups arrived earlier. Archaeologists have found arrowheads dating from about 10,000 to 9000 BCE.

These early peoples found that California was a wonderful place to live. Huge lakes—created by the melting ice—covered vast areas that are now desert. The climate was mild, and food was plentiful, so they settled down and stayed.

California's "First Settlers"

Archaeologists discovered arrowheads in California thought to be between 11,000 and 12,000 years old. They believed the arrowheads were similar to those found near Folsom and Clovis, New Mexico. Thus the ancient Californians who made the arrowheads are called the Folsom/Clovis people. The arrowheads were found near Clear Lake in Lake County and near Tulare Lake in Kings County. The arrowheads have a channel cut down the center so that they could be mounted on a wooden shaft.

Ancient Petroglyphs and Pictographs

Petroglyphs and **pictographs** appear on the walls of remote canyons and caves in many parts of California. Petroglyphs are carvings in rock, and pictographs are paintings on rock. The oldest petroglyphs are at least 3,000 years old. Pictographs are more recent, dating from about 500 CE. Most of these ancient works of art are found in the southern California lands of the Chumash and Panamint Shoshone peoples.

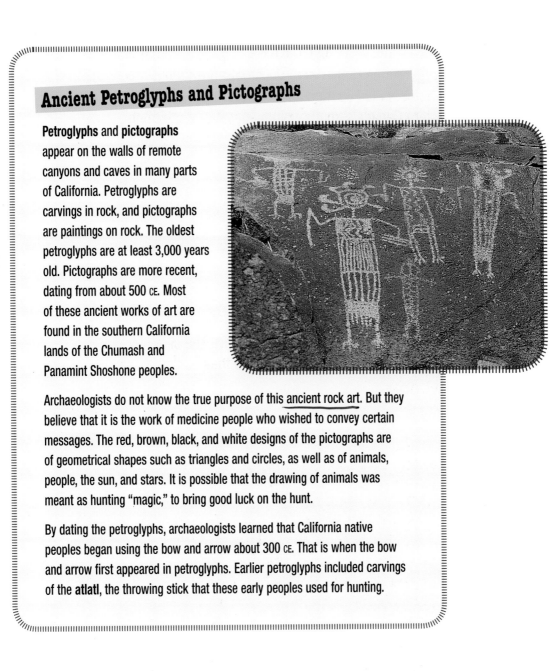

Archaeologists do not know the true purpose of this ancient rock art. But they believe that it is the work of medicine people who wished to convey certain messages. The red, brown, black, and white designs of the pictographs are of geometrical shapes such as triangles and circles, as well as of animals, people, the sun, and stars. It is possible that the drawing of animals was meant as hunting "magic," to bring good luck on the hunt.

By dating the petroglyphs, archaeologists learned that California native peoples began using the bow and arrow about 300 CE. That is when the bow and arrow first appeared in petroglyphs. Earlier petroglyphs included carvings of the **atlatl**, the throwing stick that these early peoples used for hunting.

For thousands of years, the native peoples of California usually lived in peace with each other. The land provided enough for everyone. Most tribes were not interested in making war on their neighbors. Fortunately, California's mountains, deserts, and rugged coast provided them with natural protection. These landforms also kept them from moving to other places, so each tribal group remained more or less in the same location.

Many Tribes and Languages

Prior to the arrival of the Spaniards in the 1500s, more than 250 different groups lived in California. The groups were small in size, compared to other peoples in North America. These groups spoke 100 separate languages and more than 300 **dialects**.

All the members of a community spoke one language. When several villages near each other all spoke the same language, they were considered a tribe. Different groups often could not understand one another.

Sometimes, Native Americans referred to themselves and other groups based on their location. Along the Klamath River in northern California, the Karok lived upstream from the Yurok. So the Karok referred to themselves as Karok, meaning "upstream." They called their neighbors Yurok, meaning "downstream."

Major Native American Tribes of California

Tribe	Language Group	Location
Cahuilla (CAH-he-ah))	Uto-Aztecan	Southern
Chumash (CHU-mash) *(Shoo-mash)*	Hokan	Southern coast
Hupa (Hoo-pah)	Athapascan	Northern coast
Maidu (MAY-doo)	Penutian	Northeast
Miwok (ME-WOK)	Penutian	Central
Modoc (MO-doc)	Penutian	Northern
Mojave (Mo-hav-ee)	Hokan	Southwestern
Pomo (PO-MO)	Hokan	Northern coast
Yokut (YO-cut)	Penutian	Central
Yuma (YOU-ma)	Hokan	Southern
Yurok (YOUR-rock)	Algonquian	Northern coast

Origins of the Names of Tribes

In most cases, California's native peoples did not have names for their tribes. This was because Native Americans saw themselves as belonging to a family or village, rather than a tribe ruled by a chief. When Europeans arrived in California, they considered all Native Americans who spoke the same language to be members of one tribe. Often, Native Americans simply referred to themselves as "the people." When Europeans heard Native Americans calling themselves *pomo* or *washo*—words that mean "people"—they began referring to those Native Americans as members of the Pomo or Washo tribes. The Spaniards often used Spanish words for tribal names, based on the location of particular native peoples. For example, *Costanos* (Costanoan people) means "coast-dwellers," and *Serranos* means "mountain-dwellers."

A member of the Yurok tribe stands with his catch on the California coast.

Village Life

Prior to the arrival of the Spaniards in the 1500s, California's native peoples lived in small villages. Each community usually consisted of about 50 to 100 people. Some tribes, such as the Maidu and Miwok communities, had several hundred people. The community was actually a large, extended family called a kinship group.

California tribes, unlike many other Native American groups, were governed by a headman rather than a chief. There were a few exceptions, such as the Mojave and Yuma, in the southeast. These two tribes were ruled by warrior chiefs. These chiefs needed to be brave and skillful fighters. While most California tribes were friendly with each other, these two tribes often fought with other groups. Therefore, the chiefs were expected to be strong leaders, and everyone had to obey them.

Pasqual was a Yuma chief.

Governing System

Most tribes had a simple governing system. Each member of the tribe obeyed the laws of his or her own village. However, these laws were not always the same as the laws of other villages of the same tribe. The laws were not written but were based on **tradition**.

Other tribes regarded the headman, the leader of the largest or wealthiest family, as the most powerful person in the village. The headman was respected by all, but he did not have much control over the group. He had no power to make new laws or change ancient traditions. Nor could he punish anyone. He rarely gave direct orders, and if he did, the people might or might not obey.

Yurok obsidian knife

The headman had a high place in the society because of his status. It was generally an inherited position. He had many items such as animal skins, **obsidian** knives, and shells. These were used as money. As a leader, the headman organized hunting and fishing activities, gave advice when asked, settled arguments, and gave extra food to villagers in need.

Pictured here is a Hupa village built on the Trinity River. A single kinship group lives in a Hupa village.

In some tribes, such as the Yurok, the headman was often a spiritual and political leader. He supervised traditional **ceremonies** and served as a healer. In the larger villages of central California, especially in the south, the headman had a **council** to help him govern. The council usually consisted of village **elders**, who were often adult relatives of the headman. The village medicine person might also be a member of the council. In the Yokuts of central California, the medicine person received his or her powers through dreams. A Yokut medicine person often tried to cure someone by sucking out diseases or draining blood from the person.

Miwok women shared the food-gathering duties with Miwok men, but played no role in tribal leadership.

When Peaceful People Went to War

Sometimes, the headmen of two villages had to meet and settle arguments between the two groups. These arguments could be over access to a group of acorn trees or hunting and fishing lands. Other problems sometimes came up. A member of one tribe might have insulted someone, stolen something from a member of the other tribe, or perhaps even committed murder. Arguments were usually settled peacefully. But on rare occasions, the two tribes went to war and a fierce battle took place. Often, both sides agreed to a symbolic battle instead. Few people got hurt in such events. The men of both tribes would toss stones at each other and shout insults. Then the two headmen would agree on a peace settlement. Both tribes would then celebrate peace with a dance.

Currency and Commerce

Native Americans in California traded or bought the things they wanted or needed. Products—skins, furs, and woven baskets— were **bartered** or offered in trade. Native Americans also bought things they wanted by paying with money.

The native peoples of California did not have metal coins or paper money. The most common form of money used was made of seashells. But only special kinds of shells were accepted as money. In order to be valuable, the "money" could not be too easy to get. The shells were strung on pieces of string. The more shells on the string, the higher its value. The "money" was worn on their clothing, necklaces, and headbands.

The **Dentalium shell**, a seashell shaped like a tooth, was the favorite type of money among the Yurok.

In central California, the most common type of money was in the form of small, flat, round discs made of clamshells. The discs, each about the size of a nickel, were strung like beads. Clamshells were common, so clamshell money was not worth as much as Dentalium shells.

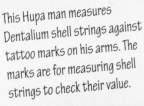

This Hupa man measures Dentalium shell strings against tattoo marks on his arms. The marks are for measuring shell strings to check their value.

This Mojave clay storage jar is an item that might have been traded with another tribe.

Trade

Native Americans often traded or bartered one item for another. The Yurok traded dried fish, salty seaweed, and shells with the Hupa in exchange for nuts, seeds, and deerskins.

Most Native Americans stayed close to home and traded with members of their own or neighboring villages. Others traveled much farther, making their living by trade.

Some tribes such as the Chumash, who lived on the southern coast of California, often traded with the Mojave, who lived in the desert far to the east. A trading network was established during the early days of Native American settlement to carry goods between the coast and inland. The Chumash also traded with the Yokut, who lived in the foothills of the Sierra Nevada.

The Chumash offered shell jewelry, animal skins, deer antlers, knives, bows and arrows, and baskets for trade. In return, they got clay pottery and red dye from the Mojave and melons, tobacco, **herbs**, salt, and black dye from the Yokut. The Yana and Atsugewi, near volcanic Mount Lassen, traded obsidian tools and arrow points in exchange for blankets and acorns with Native Americans farther south.

Living with the Environment

California has many different **environments**, probably more than any other part of North America. In order to survive in the region, native peoples had to adapt to these various environments. They had to use the land for food, shelter, and clothing.

Living off the Land

California's native peoples were mostly hunters and gatherers. Variety in their diets matched the variety in environments. Although Native Americans could not choose from as many products as in a modern supermarket, at least 500 different foods were available. The main food in the native diet was the acorn. It was nutritious, and it was readily available in most parts of California. A single, large oak tree was capable of producing up to 454 kilograms (1,000 pounds) of acorns a year. Native American women harvested the acorns and stored them in large baskets.

The only Native Americans to develop the farming and **irrigation** of crops were the Yuma in the desert along the Colorado River. Acorns and other foods found easily elsewhere were unavailable in the desert. They planted beans, pumpkins, watermelons, wheat, cantaloupes, and a type of corn called maize.

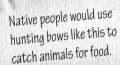

Native people would use hunting bows like this to catch animals for food.

The Hupa, Yurok, Karok, Shasta, Tolowa, Wiyot, and Wailaki peoples of northwestern California adapted well to their rainy environment. They lived in settlements along the river banks and along the Pacific coast. They ate mostly salmon and other fish, mussels and other shellfish, acorns, elk, and deer. The Shasta mixed dry, powdered berries with **meal** to sweeten it. They also stored pine nuts for the winter.

In northeastern California, the Modoc, Achomawi, and Atsugewi peoples ate salmon, deer, rabbits, grass seeds, roots, and water lily seeds. The valleys, hills, and central Californian coast were home to the Miwok, Costanoan, Pomo, and Esselen peoples.

Acorns must be specially prepared before being eaten. In the picture above, a Native American woman is drying acorns.

Cooking with Acorns

Before anyone could eat the acorns, a bitter chemical called tannin had to be removed. Using a flat stone, women ground the acorn into a flour. They then rinsed the flour several times with hot water, often in a finely-woven basket, which removed the tannin. The flour was then made into a thick porridge by mixing it with water in a watertight cooking basket. The mixture was then cooked by dropping hot stones into it. The resulting acorn mush, something like hot cereal, was usually eaten plain, but sometimes honey or berries were added to sweeten it. Sometimes acorn flour was made into a flat piece of bread and baked in the fire.

Fry bread, made of flour, baking powder, and salt, is still a staple food for many Native Americans.

In the inland mountains and valleys were the Maidu, Wintun, Yokuts, Yana, and Monache people. The diet of these groups consisted of salmon, acorns, deer, elk, antelope, rabbits, and birds. In addition to salmon and acorns, the Pomo and Costanoan ate mussels and other shellfish. The Maidu also ate eel, grasshoppers, caterpillars, and the eggs of yellow jackets.

In the high desert country east of the Sierra Nevada, lakes such as Mono Lake were too **alkaline** to support fish. So the Mono Paiute people ate kutsavi, the **larva** of a fly, found on the shores of Mono Lake. Kutsavi was rich in protein. The diet of the Chemehuevi, Panamint Shoshone (also called Koso), Kawaiisu, and Serrano peoples of the deserts of southern California included cactus fruit, seeds, flowers, and piñon pine nuts. They also ate lizards, ground squirrels, skunks, porcupines, raccoons, rabbits, and mountain sheep.

Taking Shelter

California has a wide variety of **climates**—from cold, rainy winters in the north to hot, dry summers in the south. The deserts have extremely hot summers. As a result, Native Americans developed practical types of housing that matched their lifestyles and could be made with the available materials.

In places such as northwestern California, food was available throughout the year for gathering and storing. As a result, people lived in the same houses year round. In other places, the land was less productive. To find food, the village group would have to move to other parts of their territory at different times of the year. In summer and fall, they gathered seeds and acorns in the hills. Because they were on the move, they built temporary houses—light, brush-covered shelters, open at the sides and held up by four poles.

Yurok and Hupa houses in the northwest were rectangular, wooden structures. The walls and roof were made of redwood or cedar wood planks. Native Americans set a fire at the base of a redwood or cedar tree to knock it down. They then split the tree into planks, or boards, with an elkhorn wedge.

People living in the deserts of southern California often ate the seeds of flowers of the Joshua tree—a plant that looks similar to a cactus.

This redwood slab house is still used by the Yurok of Patrick's Point State Park near Eureka, California.

The Shasta people lived east of the Yurok and Hupa. Winters there were colder than along the coast. So for extra warmth, the Shasta built their houses in a deep hole in the ground. A wooden plank roof was placed over it.

The Yuki, Pomo, and Miwok to the south, and groups in the Sacramento Valley to the east, built cone-shaped houses made of slabs of bark. Its cone shape made the tepee easy to fold and transport. Native American tribes would often transport the tepee by dragging it behind a horse. They also built wood-frame houses that were thatched with grass and covered with earth.

This tepee, made of tree bark, is one example of a typical Miwok home.

In the northeast, the Modoc had underground, earth-covered brush houses. The Achomawi had an underground bark house that was entered from the roof. The Washo, in the Lake Tahoe area of the Sierra Nevada, built dome-shaped houses thatched with **tule**, leaves, or bark. In the deserts of southern California, houses were often nothing more than simple shelters from the sun. The Cahuilla built square or oblong houses with mat roofs and walls plastered with mud. Mojave houses consisted of a frame of poles, thatched and covered with sand.

Native American dwellings in California varied in size from very small to homes large enough to sleep several families. There were also two special types of California Native American structures—the roundhouse and the sweat house. The roundhouses of the Maidu, Miwok, and other central California people were used for religious **ceremonies**. Sweat houses were dome-shaped or cone-shaped, and usually covered with earth. These houses were mainly for men, except on special occasions when women were allowed inside. A fire was built inside, and since there was no hole for smoke to escape, it became hot and smoky. Men gathered there in the evenings, and often slept there, away from their families.

Native American men gathered in sweat houses either for private talks or for cleansing and healing rituals.

Native American Clothing

What the native people of California wore depended on the season and weather. In warm weather, the men wore very little—a strip of animal skin wrapped around the hips—or nothing at all. The women wore two-piece fringed skirts made of animal skin or plant fibers and a tightly woven, round cap on their head.

Men and women decorated their faces and bodies with painted designs and tattoos. Women wore bead and shell necklaces, and hairbands and belts made of birds' feathers. The men wore necklaces of birds' beaks, animal teeth, or shells.

Native Americans usually went barefoot. But they wore deerskin moccasins on hunting and food-gathering trips. Native people in the southern deserts wore open sandals made of woven yucca fibers to protect their feet against the burning sands. In the Sierra Nevada, the Modoc and Maidu used wooden snowshoes.

This Karok woman is making baskets. She is wearing a **traditional** hat and skirt of her tribe.

To keep warm in winter, the Modoc wore leggings made of woven tule fibers. The Costanoan wore a rabbit-skin coat during the day and used it as a blanket at night. As protection against cold or wet weather, most native peoples used deerskin blankets as capes.

California Native American Basket-Weaving

Native American women throughout California made baskets for every purpose and occasion. There were 1.5-meter- (5-foot-) tall baskets for storing acorns, baskets for carrying firewood, baskets for trapping animals, baskets to carry infants, and gift baskets. There were even basketry items of clothing, such as hats, belts, and sandals.

There were two basic basket-making techniques. There was a form of weaving called **twining**, and a stitched form known as **coiling**. Native American mothers taught basket weaving and design to their daughters. Therefore, the designs of each family group remained pretty much the same from generation to generation. The baskets were made from various plant fibers. The fibers could be colored red, yellow, and black using plant dyes from blackberries, sunflowers, buttercups, elderberries, and the indigo bush. Pomo women were considered to be the best basket makers in California. They wove brightly colored birds' feathers into their tightly woven baskets. Their beautiful baskets became highly prized items of trade, and are still made today. The Pomo basket shown here is a large gift basket.

Rituals, Customs, and Beliefs

The origins of some **rituals**, **customs**, and spiritual beliefs of California's native peoples is lost in time. The Native Americans, just like all other peoples in the world, sought the meaning of life and an understanding of their world. For thousands of years, these spiritual beliefs have been passed down from one generation to the next. Many are still practiced today.

Creation Myths

Three important religious systems developed among the native peoples of California—World Renewal in northwestern California, Kuksu in central California, and Toloache farther south. Each religion had its own secret **traditional** beliefs, **ceremonies**, and rituals. All Native American groups believed in the Creator—a supreme being who created the world.

Some believed that the Creator was an animal. The Yokut believed the coyote created human beings. Others believed the Creator had a humanlike form. The Maidu called the Creator "Earth Maker." The Cahto people in northern California called the Creator "Thunder God." Creation stories explained how the world came to be.

World Renewal people such as the Hupa believe that the Creator renews the world each year. The group performs rituals that it believes will prevent famine.

Hupa participants in the White Deer Dance display items that indicate their wealth.

All Native American groups believed that everything in the world has a spirit. Animals, birds, plants, mountains, winds, and water each contain a spirit that can talk. However, Native Americans believed most humans could not understand spirit languages.

Religious Systems

Once a year, the World Renewal groups held ceremonies honoring the Creator, so that the Creator would once again fill the oak trees with acorns and the rivers with salmon. Native Americans of different tribes from several villages would gather at a host village for ceremonies that often lasted two weeks.

World Renewal religious practices, overseen by a medicine person, involved the performance of special songs and dances. Usually only the men took part in the rituals, while the women watched.

Hupa and Karok dancers wore decorated costumes, such as skins from the rare white albino deer. White deer dancers also carried poles, around which they draped deerskins. The Hupa and Karok performed these ritual dances to prevent famine and natural disasters and to ensure that there were enough natural resources.

These Miwok dancers were part of a **traditional** festival still performed today.

In a ritual called the Jumping Dance, dancers imitated the crouching and leaping movements of animals. World Renewal ceremonies were social events as well. Families met people of other villages. Men gathered in the sweat house and competed in athletic events. Wealthy families displayed their possessions.

The Pomo, Maidu, Costanoan, and Miwok of central California practiced Kuksu. *Kuksu* was the name of a Pomo spirit. Like the World Renewal Creator, Kuksu renewed the plants and animals that gave life to the believers. Kuksu villages took turns hosting yearly, week-long Kuksu ceremonies. But Kuksu dances and costumes were different from the World Renewal ceremonies. Robes and feathered headdresses were worn, and they danced in the village roundhouse. The dancers pretended to be Kuksu and other spirits through their movements. Boys took part in secret **initiation** ceremonies, where the medicine person would teach the customs of adulthood.

Southern California peoples such as the Yokut, Luiseño, and Cahuilla believed in Toloache. *Toloache* is Spanish for "jimsonweed," a desert plant with white bell-like flowers. During a tribal initiation, boys drank a mixture of water and jimsonweed root.

Some native peoples believed the jimsonweed was a plant of the gods and should not be touched.

Ritual Music

Most ceremonies involved dancing and music. Singing usually took the form of chanting in time to hand clapping and foot stomping. Simple musical instruments were used, especially rattles. One rattle was made by fastening two turtle shells together, with pebbles or cherry pits inside. Another rattle, like the one shown here, was made by tying several dry deer hooves to a stick. Yet another was made by putting pebbles inside dried insect cocoons tied to a stick. A clapper rattle, used by the Maidu, was made by half-splitting a stick and wrapping it so the two halves clapped or rattled together.

A foot-drum was used by the Indians of central California. A flat wooden plank or a large hollowed-out log was set over a hole in the floor of the roundhouse. It was sounded by a man pounding on it in rhythm with his heels while dancing. Indians also used a wooden whistle at ceremonies. Its shrill sounds were so piercing that it was easily heard above the chanting and drumming.

Coming-of-Age Rituals

When Native American boys and girls reached the age at which they became young adults, they took part in coming-of-*age rituals.* The various tribes marked this event in different ways. But the purpose of this ritual was the same for each group. It was meant to give the young person strength to deal with the hardships of life.

Boys of the Luiseño people of southern California underwent a particularly difficult test. At the age of 18, a boy had to lie in a pit and allow ants to crawl over him. He could not flinch or show pain. In this way, Native Americans believed the boy gained power to overcome harm from arrows.
Girls of southern California tribes came of age earlier than boys, often being married by age 15. So when she turned 13 or 14, a girl took part in a "roasting" ritual. The girl had to lie on her back with hot rocks on her abdomen in a pit of sand for four days and three nights. It was thought that this would make her strong enough to endure childbearing and other hardships.

They would then fall asleep for many hours. The plant caused them to dream or have a vision. The vision gave the boys a kind of power, making them braver or stronger. When they awoke, the medicine person and the village **elders** made a sand painting on the ground, using earth and sand of different colors. The designs they created showed things from nature such as wolves, snakes, spiders, the sun, the moon, and the stars. The medicine person used the painting to teach the boys about the natural and spirit world. At the end of the lesson, the painting was destroyed.

Medicine People

The medicine person in most California tribes was, along with the headman or chief, the most powerful person in the village. This person's main job was to heal the sick. Medicine people were also religious leaders and gave the headman or chief advice on many matters. In California, native people also relied on the medicine person for such tasks as predicting weather and naming children.

Medicine people had special abilities. Some could predict the future. A medicine person might be called upon to make it rain. Some people believed that medicine people could turn into a bear and kill their enemies. Nobody knew the limits of a medicine person's power, but people believed that power could be used for both good and evil.

A medicine person had to go through many years of training. A child usually began training after having a dream about a spiritual being. This being then became the young person's guardian spirit.

An experienced medicine person taught the young person methods of healing and special rituals. A medicine person often used **herbs** and other plants to cure diseases or injuries such as rattlesnake bites. Once the student developed skills, he or she would be recognized in an initiation ceremony that included **fasting** and a special dance.

Unlike most other tribes, most Hupa, Yurok, and Karok medicine people were women.

Outside Influences

The native peoples of California lived at peace in their own world for thousands of years—following their age-old **traditional** ways of life. But something happened that would prove to be a **catastrophe** for the California native peoples—the arrival of Europeans.

California Missions

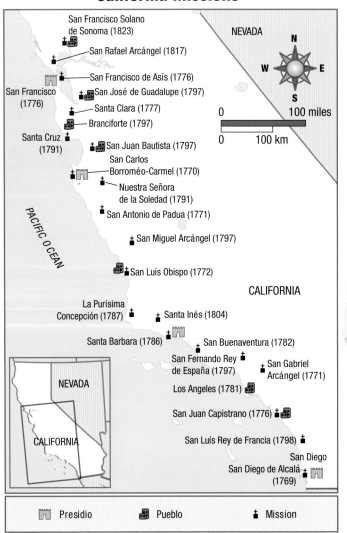

There were 21 missions in the area we now know as California. Presidios and pueblos were often built near the missions.

On this map, the dates in parentheses tell what year the mission, presidio, or pueblo was built.

Chumash priests are thought to have made these cave paintings to ask supernatural beings and forces to help in their daily lives.

The Mission Culture

In 1492 Christopher Columbus brought news of a new land back to Europe. The Spaniards, who had paid for Columbus's exploration, quickly **colonized** the Caribbean and parts of South America. In 1542 Juan Cabrillo sailed north from New Spain—which is now Mexico—in search of gold. Reaching the coast of present-day southern California, he encountered the Chumash. Cabrillo thus became the first European to see California's native peoples. In 1602 the Spanish explorer Sebastian Vizcaino mapped the California coast. Europeans did not visit again for the next 167 years.

Then, in 1769, Father Junípero Serra and a few other **Franciscan padres** traveled north from New Spain to what is now San Diego and established a **mission** there. Spain encouraged the building of missions and **forts** in California. Spain wanted to convert the native people to **Christianity**, as well as take over their territory. The Franciscan padres eventually built 21 missions. The string of missions along the California coast went as far north as Sonoma, near San Francisco.

When the missions were built, the natives in nearby villages usually welcomed the Spaniards in friendship. The padres encouraged the native people to live at the missions. They were drawn to the missions in hopes of conducting trade.

The Native Americans entered the missions willingly, at first. But once there, they were forced to work for the Spaniards for very little in return. They grew products such as wheat, olives, and grapes. The men were also trained in tile making, carpentry, leatherwork, blacksmithing, and **masonry**. The women worked at spinning and weaving yarn, making clothing, and baking bread.

The Native Americans received religious training from the padres and were baptized as **Catholics**. They were forced to give up many of their traditional **customs**. They had to learn Spanish and stop using their native languages. Often native peoples from different villages lived in the same mission. The padres named the group according to the mission to which they belonged, such as *Diegueños* at Mission San Diego and *Gabrieliños* at Mission San Gabriel.

When mission leaders prayed, they expected the Native Americans to take part, too.

Life was rough for the native people living in the missions. They were not used to long hours of labor. Even worse, they were not free to leave. Native Americans who did not obey or tried to escape were severely punished. Sometimes they were even killed to serve as a warning to others.

Native Americans faced other problems at the missions, too. The missions were dirty and overcrowded. The native people were not used to the different foods. Worst of all, they caught European diseases brought by the Spaniards. Many died from measles, smallpox, and other diseases.

Native Americans staged **revolts** over the years at some of the missions. In 1775 about 600 *Diegueño* people burned the Mission San Diego and killed a padre. In 1824 about 2,000 Native Americans attacked Mission La Purisma. That same year, the mission at Santa Barbara was burned by Native Americans. But despite these attempts, the Native Americans were unable to overthrow the mission system.

Mission Santa Barbara is solid brick and stone, with walls 1.8 meters (6 feet) thick. The huge red tiles of the roof also reflect long-lasting workmanship.

The Missions End

Meanwhile, in 1821, Mexico had won its independence from Spain. In 1834 the Mexican government ordered the California missions to be torn down. From then on, each mission chapel would simply become a local **Catholic** church.

With the ending of the mission system, each adult male Native American living in a mission was to receive 13 hectares (33 acres) of mission land. Unfortunately, many Native Americans were not told about these rights. Most of the land went to wealthy *rancheria* owners.

The mission Native Americans had few options. They could work for the *rancheria* owners or work in the nearby towns where cheap labor was in demand. Wherever they decided to work, they were treated no better than slaves. Some went back inland, far from white people's towns and *rancherias* near the coast. They tried to live again in the traditions of their **ancestors**. They joined existing Native American communities or formed new ones. But as the years went by, European communities grew larger, and soon, the difficult situation of the native peoples would become even worse.

This former mission is in ruins, either as a result of a Native American attack or due to orders from the Mexican government to tear down the missions.

During the gold rush, many Native Americans had to move to places like this rancheria in Yuba City, California.

The Gold Rush

In January 1848, gold was discovered at Sutter's Mill, near present-day Sacramento. Soon after, thousands of **prospectors** came to the gold fields of California, hoping to get rich. Groups of Native Americans lived in the hills of the gold country. In 1848 half the people looking for gold were Native Americans, hired by the owners of *rancherias*. But the large number of newcomers in the area eventually led to problems. Many of the newcomers had no respect for the rights of the native people. The gold miners trespassed on native hunting grounds, killing animals, chopping down trees, and filling salmon streams with **silt**. The main food sources of Native Americans were soon destroyed.

The Killing Begins

Spanish missionaries had not treated the Native Americans as equals, and people now flooding into California did not show any respect toward the natives. Before long, the killing began. In 1849 five men were missing from a mining camp. The Native Americans were blamed, even though there was no evidence. A gang of white men entered a Native American village and killed about 100 people. This and other violent acts caused the Native Americans to leave for other parts of California. But the violence continued whenever they encountered white people. Later that year, U.S. soldiers attacked a Pomo village at Clear Lake, killing 135 Pomo.

Peter Burnett

In 1851 California governor Peter Burnett announced that "a war of **extermination** will continue to be waged between the races until the Indian race becomes **extinct**." Following this, settlers offered **bounties** for the scalps or heads of Native Americans. By 1860 gangs had killed thousands of natives. The killing continued for more than ten years. During this time, many more Native Americans died from disease and starvation.

If a Native American dared to steal a horse or some food, his whole family was often killed. Gangs of whites roamed through California, kidnapping Native American children and young women to sell as **indentured servants**. An estimated 3,000 to 4,000 Native American children were taken from their families in this way. Often, their parents were killed. The California law that legalized this form of slavery was not **repealed** until 1863.

Broken Promises

After California joined the Union in 1850, the federal government became involved in the new state's affairs. The government wanted to bring order to the region and make use of its **resources**. Three **commissioners** were sent to California to study the situation. They learned that most white citizens wanted all Native Americans out of California. But there was no place to send them.

The commissioners' first priority was to end the conflict between the people in California. They negotiated 18 treaties with various groups of Native Americans. The Native Americans gave up all **claim** to the territories, agreeing to recognize U.S. government ownership of California. They promised not to attack U.S. citizens. In return, the commissioners promised that about 3 million hectares (7.5 million acres), a small portion of the state, would be set aside for Native Americans to use. They also promised to provide food, clothing, livestock, and tools, as well as help from teachers, farmers, and others.

However, in June 1852, the U.S. Senate rejected the commissioners' agreements with the native peoples. California's Native Americans became landless, with no rights of citizenship or protection under the law. The government set up 10,000-hectare (25,000-acre) farms on land no one else wanted. Native Americans were moved to farms where the soil was poor, there was little water, and there were few animals for them to hunt.

Members of the Paiute, Pachanga, and Cahuilla tribes met with a government official in 1937, hoping for better treatment.

Not surprisingly, the farms failed. Native Americans were not given tools and training as had been promised. Many starved. Eventually, many people left the farms. The government then set up **reservations**. Native Americans were unhappy when they were moved to a place far from their homeland. One tribe, the Hupa, fought for five years to remain on their land. Finally, in 1864, they were given a reservation on their homelands in the Hoopa Valley. However, other Native Americans were less fortunate. In April 1870, the Modoc returned to their homeland in northeastern California. The resulting war with the U.S. Army ended with the Modoc's defeat in 1873. This was the last major battle between white settlers and California's Native Americans.

During the late 1800s, the conditions on the remaining reservations were terrible. Many suffered from poverty, disease, and lack of food. In addition, reservation officials discouraged Native Americans from keeping their traditions and **culture**. Many Native Americans left. They struggled to survive by taking low-paying jobs in agriculture, ranching, or mining. Land ownership was not possible for most.

The Ghost Dance

In 1870 Tavivo, a medicine person of the Paiutes in western Nevada, described a vision. In Tavivo's vision, all white people would be destroyed, and the ghosts of the dead Native Americans would return and reclaim their homelands. Word of Tavivo's vision spread to Native Americans throughout the West. Those Native Americans who had suffered the greatest losses, such as the Pomo, Maidu, and Yokut, became the most enthusiastic of Tavivo's followers. They gathered in roundhouses and performed a special **ritual** known as the Ghost Dance.

California Natives Today

This roundhouse is still used today by the Miwok.

In the early part of the 1900s, various organizations were formed to try to right the wrongs that had been done to California's native peoples. Early efforts focused on improving educational opportunities for Native American children. The struggle to get back rights and lands also began. One important goal was achieved in 1924, when all Native Americans born in the United States were granted citizenship. Finally, California's Native Americans had the right to vote and to hold elected office.

The Right to Own Land

Federal government policy regarding land for Native Americans was often **contradictory**. On the one hand, the government wanted to get rid of all responsibility for Native Americans by giving back some land. The Dawes Act of 1887 forced parts of reservation lands to go to private families. On the other hand, the government eventually wanted to "civilize" the Native Americans. The reservation was a place where help could be given in the form of housing, education, and medical benefits.

Current Indian Reservations

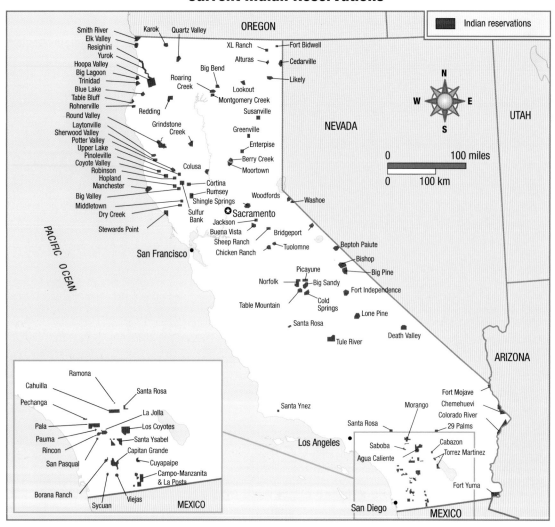

The Indian Reorganization Act of 1934 ended further distribution of reservation lands. The government encouraged members of tribes to come together again as a group. Congress provided additional lands for California Native Americans, but only if they would adopt the government style of the United States. By 1950 the federal government had set up 117 Native American communities. These **reservations** and *rancherias* varied from an 0.4-hectare (1-acre) plot in Strawberry Valley within Yuba County, to the 46,944-hectare (116,000-acre) Hoopa Reservation in Humboldt County.

There are 107 federally-recognized Native American tribes and about 100 federal Native American reservations in the state of California, with about 40 Native American groups seeking to gain federal recognition.

Challenging the Government

California Native Americans had also been waging a struggle to be paid for the lands that had been lost to white settlers during the 1800s. In the 1920s, the **Mission** Indian Federation, the California Indian Brotherhood, and the California Indian Rights Association sued the federal government for not **ratifying** the 18 treaties of 1852. That legal battle took 16 years to reach an end. The Native Americans of California were awarded $17 million. However, $12 million was subtracted to pay for services the federal government had provided to the Native Americans over the years. The Native Americans really won only $5 million—about $150 to each of 36,000 Native Americans whose names had been approved.

In 1946 Congress created the Indian Claims Commission. California Native Americans filed several additional lawsuits. In 1963 the Native Americans agreed to a settlement of $29.1 million. In 1972 the government approved giving $700 per person to 69,000 Native Americans. The cash awards could not even begin to make up for all that was lost, but at least the government had been forced to accept responsibility for past wrongs.

A Native American woman weaves a basket on the Hoopa Reservation in Humboldt County, California.

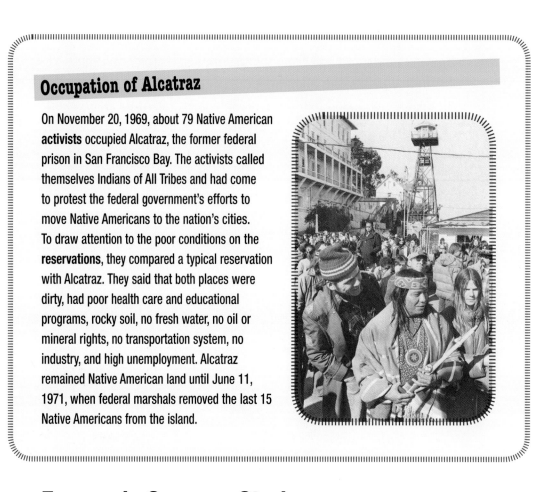

Occupation of Alcatraz

On November 20, 1969, about 79 Native American **activists** occupied Alcatraz, the former federal prison in San Francisco Bay. The activists called themselves Indians of All Tribes and had come to protest the federal government's efforts to move Native Americans to the nation's cities. To draw attention to the poor conditions on the **reservations**, they compared a typical reservation with Alcatraz. They said that both places were dirty, had poor health care and educational programs, rocky soil, no fresh water, no oil or mineral rights, no transportation system, no industry, and high unemployment. Alcatraz remained Native American land until June 11, 1971, when federal marshals removed the last 15 Native Americans from the island.

Economic Success Stories: Water Rights

The Mojave have a **claim** to water rights on the Colorado River in the desert at the southeastern corner of California. The Mojave have found economic success by leasing **irrigated** land to large agricultural businesses. About 33,445 hectares (100,000 acres) of desert land are now being farmed at the Colorado River Reservation. The land is irrigated by a system of 402 kilometers (250 miles) of canals.

Farther south along the Colorado River, at Lake Havasu, is the Chemehuevi Reservation. The Chemehuevi have spent millions of dollars for tourists on their reservation land. Amenities include marinas, a motel, campgrounds, a restaurant, a store, and a passenger ferry.

Preserving Native Culture and Traditions

California tribes that remained on their **traditional** lands have been the most successful at preserving their Native American traditions. In many parts of California, Native Americans continue to preserve their **culture**. The history of a people remains a part of who the people are. By speaking their native languages and performing their traditional **ceremonies**, they keep their culture alive and move forward as a people.

Gambling

The **gambling** business is a huge new source of income for Native American tribes. The value of the business in many places has increased because customers lose several billion dollars a year at the casinos. And what the customer loses, the tribe gains. The casino shown below is the Viejas Indian Casino in San Diego.

Although the Indian Gaming Regulatory Act of 1988 recognized that tribes have the right to control gaming, tribes are required to negotiate with the state how some types of gaming are handled. Most tribes do not want any state control, because reservations are supposed to be beyond the control of state laws. Each federally recognized Native American tribe functions as an independent nation within the territory of the United States.

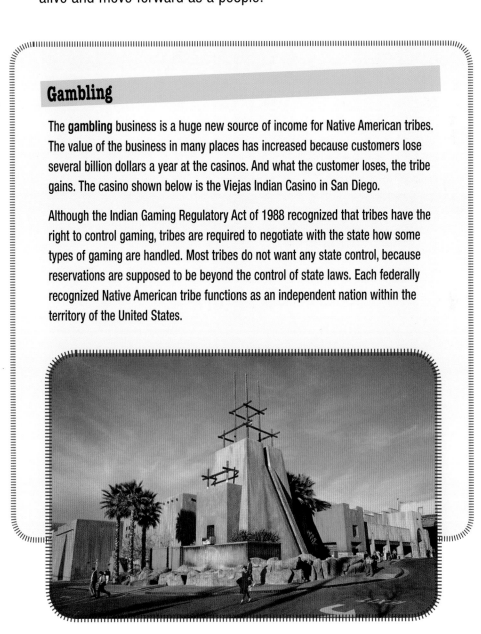

Map of California

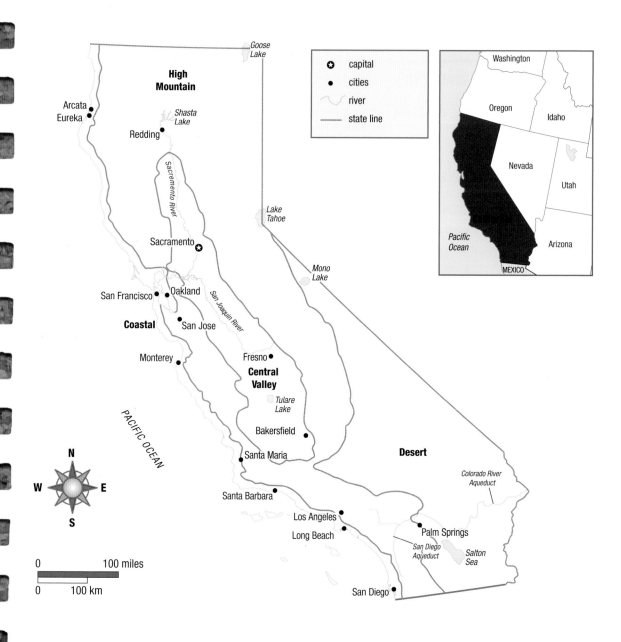

Legend:
- ✪ capital
- • cities
- ～ river
- — state line

Map labels:

High Mountain

Goose Lake

Arcata
Eureka

Shasta Lake

Redding

Sacramento River

Lake Tahoe

Sacramento ✪

Mono Lake

San Francisco • • Oakland

Coastal

San Jose

San Joaquin River

Monterey

Fresno •

Central Valley

Tulare Lake

Bakersfield

Santa Maria

Desert

Colorado River Aqueduct

PACIFIC OCEAN

Santa Barbara

Los Angeles •
Long Beach

Palm Springs

San Diego Aqueduct

Salton Sea

San Diego •

N
W E
S

0   100 miles

0   100 km

Inset map:

Washington

Oregon

Idaho

Nevada

Utah

Pacific Ocean

Arizona

MEXICO

Timeline

9000–10,000
The first Paleo-Indians live in what is now California.

6000–8000
Most groups of California native peoples settle in California.

300 CE The bow and arrow first appear in California **petroglyphs**.

1492 CE Christopher Columbus discovers the New World.

1521 Hernán Cortés conquers the Aztecs in what is now Mexico. Spain establishes the colony of New Spain.

1542 Juan Cabrillo reaches the coast of southern California and encounters the Chumash.

1579 Sir Francis Drake reaches the coast of northern California and encounters Coast Miwok.

1769 Father Junípero Serra establishes Mission San Diego.

1775 Diegueño people burn down Mission San Diego.

1821 Mexico wins independence from Spain.

1824 Native Americans attack Mission La Purisma and several others.

1834 Mexico orders the end of **missions**.

1848 Gold is discovered at Sutter's Mill near present-day Sacramento. The gold rush begins (January). The United States and Mexico sign the Treaty of Guadalupe Hidalgo. The United States gains California and other areas (February).

1849 Widespread violence by whites against Native Americans begins. Native Americans flee the gold country.

1851 California governor Peter Burnett announces a "war of **extermination**" against Indians.

1852 The U.S. Senate refuses to **ratify** 18 treaties negotiated with Native Americans in June.

1873 The Modoc are defeated by the U.S. Army in June, in the last major battle between whites and Native Americans in California.

1924 All Native Americans born in the United States are granted citizenship that includes the right to vote and hold elected office.

1920s Native Americans sue the federal government for failing to ratify the treaties of 1852, which results in the payment of $150 per person.

1934 Indian Reorganization Act ends further distribution of **reservation** lands.

1946 The U.S. Congress creates the Indian Claims Commission.

1963 Native Americans agree to a second settlement, paying $700 a person.

1969 Native Americans occupy Alcatraz Island in San Francisco Bay in November to protest government policies and poor conditions on reservations. This ends in June 1971.

1988 U.S. government passes Indian Gaming Regulatory Act.

1998 California Assembly passes a bill making Native American Day (4th Friday in September) an official state holiday.

Glossary

activist someone who publicly supports a cause

alkaline having a bitter taste and reacting with acid to form salt

ancestor one from whom an individual has descended

archaeologist person who studies history through the things that people have made or built

atlatl throwing stick used by Indians for hunting

barter to trade one thing for another without using money

bounty money given as a reward for capturing people or animals

catastrophe sudden disaster

Catholic one who belongs to the Catholic Church, the branch of Christianity centered in Rome

ceremony act performed according to fixed rules

Christianity religion based on the life and teachings of Jesus Christ

claim ownership

climate weather conditions in a certain area

coiling type of stitching used by California Indians in making baskets

colonized came to one land from another and took control

commissioner person given a specific task by the government

contradictory opposite of something else

council group that meets to make important decisions and give advice

culture ideas, skills, arts, and a way of life of a certain people at a certain time

custom usual way of doing things

Dentalium shell tooth-shaped seashell used as money by California Indians

dialect form of language belonging to a certain region

elder older person who helps lead a community

environment surroundings

extermination killing off all members of a group in a location

extinct no longer living

fasting going without food for a cause or purpose

fort strong building used for defense against enemy attack

Franciscan priest dedicated to preaching, missions, and charities

gamble play a game in which something is risked

glacier large body of ice moving slowly over a wide area of land

herb plant with parts that are used as medicine or to flavor food

Ice Age period of colder climate when much of North America was covered by thick glaciers

indentured servant person who is bound to work for another for a specified time

initiation ceremony in which someone is admitted into a group

irrigation supply water to land

land bridge land connecting Alaska and Siberia during last Ice Age when the sea level was much lower

larva wingless form in which many insects are born

masonry building with stone, brick, or concrete

meal coarsely ground seeds made into a paste

mission church community set up by traveling priests called missionaries

nomadic hunter hunter who moved from place to place following the herds of wild animals

obsidian black volcanic glass

padre Spanish word for priest

petroglyph ancient carving in rock

pictograph ancient painting in rock

prospector person who explores a region in search of valuable minerals

rancheria small reservation, usually large enough only for houses and tiny garden plots (originally a Spanish word for "Indian village")

ratify give legal approval

repeal do away with by legal action

reservation tract of public land set aside for use by American Indians

resource something that is available to take care of a need; there are natural and human-made resources

revolt rebel against authority

ritual words and actions of a religious ceremony; religious rites

silt particles left in water

tradition custom of belief handed down from generation to generation

tule type of plant similar to cattails

twining type of weaving used by California Indians in making baskets

Find Out More

Books

Behrens, June. *Central Coast Missions in California*. Minneapolis, MN: Lerner Publications, 2008.

Orr, Tamra B. *California*. Danbury, CT: Children's Press, 2007.

Rosinsky, Natalie M. *The Chumash and Their History*. Mankato, MN: Compass Point Books, 2005.

Williams, Jack. *The Mojave of California.* New York: Rosen Publishing, 2004.

Websites

http://www.californiahistory.org/

This site, designed by a teacher, provides photos, links, and a detailed timeline about California's rich history (from its exploration through the Gold Rush).

http://ceres.ca.gov/ceres/calweb/native.html

This site lists some of the state's many tribes of Native Americans and provides links to cultural resources.

Index